English and Maths in Your Pocket

An A-Z of ideas for developing English and maths in every lesson

Dan Williams, 2015

ISBN 978-1-326-27563-1

This pocket book will provide you with an A-Z of simple and effective ways to develop maths and English in every lesson.

Dan Williams (@FurtherEdagogy) is a Teaching and Learning Coach at a large General Further Education College in the Midlands. A self-confessed edu-geek, Dan has always looked to implement innovative techniques to develop the English and maths skills of learners within vocational lessons.

Dan believes that the time has come to ditch the expression 'embed English and maths', in favour of more meaningful and focussed development of these core skills. After a number of years teaching and supporting teachers, he has acquired an array of ideas which have been put together in one accessible pocket book for teachers and trainers in all subjects.

"We are all teachers of English and maths"

Foreword

As a Teaching and Learning professional with an English specialism and background, THE question I most often hear is: "How do I get English into my lessons?" This question comes from all kinds of teachers teaching different subjects and vocations to vastly different learners. As Dan Williams shows, I think, marvellously in this pocketbook, we CAN develop our students' English skills in a way that is relevant and engaging without 'crowbarring' English into our lessons.

One of the things that is always worth remembering is that, whilst helping our learners develop their subject-based skills, whether that is fixing cars or dispensing pharmaceuticals, we also have a responsibility, as holistic practitioners, to help them with other skills as well. And when we talk about helping our students with their English skills, we are talking about helping them to become better listeners, better speakers, better presenters, better note-takers and better readers. The development of these essential English skills is a very important part of our role as responsible and forward-thinking teachers who are transforming learners into employable and well-rounded, competitive individuals, ready to succeed in the future.

So how do we do this? How do we find easy, engaging ways of integrating ideas into our sessions in order to develop these English skills in our learners? This easy-to-use pocket book offers 26 different, wonderfully-practical ideas for doing just this. Open the book randomly and I guarantee that you'll find a fantastic idea, written in succinct language, with a handy practical example written right next to it. The 'in a nutshell' concept of this book works brilliantly for teachers who are massively time-poor (so that's all of us!) and the examples used are from a wide variety of FE contexts. Most of all, the ideas in here are enjoyable to use and are sure to engage all learners, no matter of what age, background or subject choice. Dip in and get going!

Janette Thompson

Contents

Articulate 2
Break the Code 4
Change the Adjective 6
Data Analysis 8
Equal to 10
Feedback 12
Graphic Representation 14
Hypothesis 16
Invoice the Lesson 18
Jumbled Sentences 20
Key Features 22
Listen Carefully 24
Match the Definition 26
Number Change 28
Old-School Timing 30
Peer SP&G Check 32
Quiz Time 34
Real or Not? 36
Scrabble 38
Twenty Word Challenge 40
Units of Measurement 42
Vocational Terms 44
Word Link 46
X'plain Yourself 48
Yin/Yang, Skim/Scan 50
Zap the Waffle 52

'Articulate'

In a nutshell:

Learners are tasked with describing a word to a peer without saying the actual word.

Example:

Amjad is teaching an Anatomy and Physiology class and is getting learners to describe different bones. He divides his class into pairs. One individual from each pair is given a bone to describe to their partner. They are not allowed to say the name of the bone, or the letter it begins with. They need to describe the type of bone, its location and other clues in order for their partner to come to the correct answer.

To challenge learners further, Amjad gives additional words that cannot be used in the descriptions.

'Break the Code'

In a nutshell:

Learners are given a series of questions to answer with a number. They answer each question before calculating the total based on given commands.

Example:

For a starter activity, James gives his Automotive learners the following to answer:

Starter Activity

1. Add the firing order of a straight-6 cylinder engine together.

2. Divide the above by the number of wheels on a Reliant Robin.

3. Multiply this by the legal limit for the minimum depth of tread on car tyres (mm).

Learners solve each question before calculating the total. For example, the answer to the above would be:

---

1 - 5 - 3 - 6 - 2 - 4 = 1 + 5 + 3 + 6 + 2 + 4 = 21

21 ÷ 3 = 7

7 x 1.6 = 11.2

'Change the Adjective'

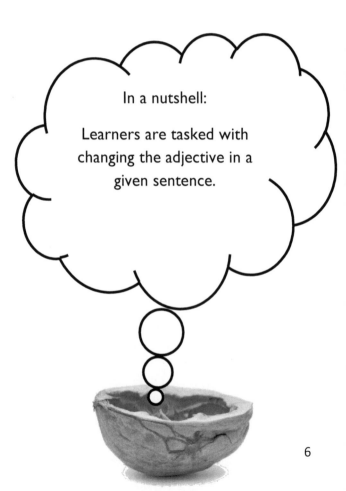

In a nutshell:

Learners are tasked with changing the adjective in a given sentence.

Example:

Joleon is teaching his Photography learners about the different types of lighting and asks each learner to describe the impact of each lighting effect on different images. Each adjective that is used by a learner must be amended by a peer. For instance, if a learner describes the image below as 'mysterious', another learner might change the adjective to 'enigmatic'. Learners could collate the adjectives with definitions for future use, thus enhancing their vocabulary.

'Data Analysis'

In a nutshell:

Learners are given data pertinent to their lesson and are required to perform an analysis of this. Alternatively, they could analyse their attendance.

Example:

Julian, an ESOL lecturer, has had some attendance issues with his learners. In a tutorial session, he provides the learners with a breakdown of attendance and punctuality. He then asks learners to calculate their percentage of attendance and set themselves targets to improve.

To extend the activity, the teacher could ask learners to calculate their maximum possible attendance percentage and then calculate the increments that they are able to make in order to set targets. For example:

> "With only 6 weeks left, it is possible to make a 2% improvement in my attendance which will take me from 78% to 80%."

E

'Equal to...'

In a nutshell:

Learners are asked to use the digits of a given number to calculate the numbers 1-10 using different operations.

Example:

Learners are given a number relevant to the lesson. For instance, Jane's Art lesson is focussed on the work of Andy Warhol. In order to assist learners with the biography, Jane uses his year of birth (1928) and asks learners to use all of the digits in the year to calculate the numbers 1-10. Learners can work independently or in small groups to complete the calculations, for example:

$$1 = (8 - 9) + 2 \times 1$$
$$2 = (1 + 8) \div 9 \times 2$$
$$3 = (9 + 2) \times 1 - 8$$
$$4 = (9 + 1 + 2) - 8$$

'Functional Problems'

In a nutshell:

Learners are given a large scale problem solving task which consolidates a range of English and maths skills.

Example:

Brian is teaching his IT learners about network storage. He provides his learners with a functional problem to solve which requires a range of skills.

As the Senior Network Manager of a college you have decided to archive electronic copies of student work.

Each student normally produces 32 GB of data over the period of a year and has access to the college network via a Username and Password Convention. In order for you to make a decision on the best way to achieve this;

1. Calculate how much storage space is required to meet the needs of 300 students.

2. Work out the size of the NAS requirement if a tolerance of 15% is considered to be a suitable overflow.

3. Calculate the cost of storage solutions both for single devices (USB) and a dedicated NAS.

4. Produce a short report of no less than 150 words to show your working and the reasons for your decision.

'Graphic Interpretation'

In a nutshell:

Learners are given relevant graphs or charts to interpret in order to illustrate important information for a session.

Example:

Dave is teaching his Public Service learners about crime rates, but rather than telling them about the change in crime rates over several decades, he provides them with a graph which they must interpret in order to explain it for themselves.

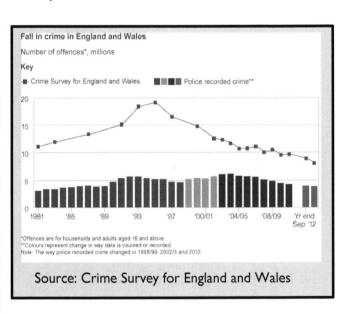

Source: Crime Survey for England and Wales

'Hypothesis'

In a nutshell:

Learners are given a scenario or situation in which they are tasked with predicting the outcome.

16

Example:

Harvey is teaching his Sport learners about nutrition and gives them the following question:

"What happens to your 'Cooper run' distance when you drink 1 litre of isotonic fluid beforehand?"

Learners must predict the outcome based on prior knowledge of the subject and during the lesson must determine whether their hypothesis was correct.

Learners may be challenged further by predicting actual differences in values. For instance in the above question, learners could predict the difference in distance with and without the fluid.

'Invoice the Lesson'

In a nutshell:

Learners need to estimate the cost of resources and labour used in a session and calculate total costs.

18

Example:

Jonathon delivers a practical Engineering class whereby learners are developing their fabrication welding skills. At the end of the session, he asks the learners to calculate the cost of the resources used and the labour costs as they would be in industry. The learners calculate the cost of the lesson based on their individual circumstances. The task can be extended with the inclusion of VAT or additional items.

'Jumbled Sentences'

In a nutshell:

Learners are given a series of jumbled words to unscramble in order to create a sentence that makes sense.

Example:

Graham is teaching his level 1 learners about healthy eating. He provides them with a jumbled sentence to rearrange in order to make sense of the topic. For instance:

sugar – only – small – eat – you – amounts – of - should

'You should only eat small amounts of sugar.'

To make the task more challenging, the teacher could add unnecessary words, so that learners have to determine which ones to include in the sentence.

'Key Features'

In a nutshell:

Learners are given a text to read related to the subject and are tasked with identifying the key features of the text.

Example:

Anton provides his Hair and Beauty learners with a topical article to read.

He then provides a series of questions related to the article.

He asks the learners to highlight the key features that are most important in order to answer the questions.

Learners then work in pairs to compare the key features and answer the given questions.

L

'Listen Carefully'

In a nutshell:

Learners need to listen to instructions or information from a peer and demonstrate that they were actively listening by paraphrasing what was said.

Example:

Stefan, a Business lecturer, asks one of his learners to answer a specific question. Upon answering the question, another learner is asked to paraphrase the answer in order to clarify that they were listening carefully. For example:

Lecturer: Sam, can you explain one aspect of the marketing mix?

Sam: Price is an aspect of marketing mix. A price is what the customer will pay to the business for a product. The cost is what it will cost them. A business needs to think carefully about the pricing strategy that they use so that they attract customers, but also make a profit.

Lecturer: Thank you. Can you paraphrase what Sam just said please, Jordan?

Jordan: Price is what people pay and cost is what the business pays. The price needs consideration in order to attract customers and make a profit.

'Match the Definition'

In a nutshell:

Learners are provided with a range of key terms and the definitions. Their task is to pair all terms and definitions correctly.

Example:

Kerri provides her IT learners with a range of key terms and definitions. Learners are tasked with matching the term and definition in order to establish the correct definitions.

To stretch the learners further, red herrings could be provided in the definition list.

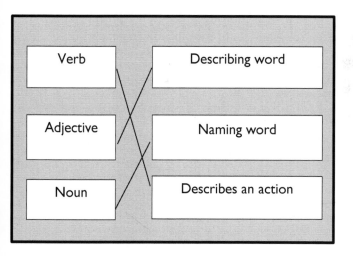

'Number Change'

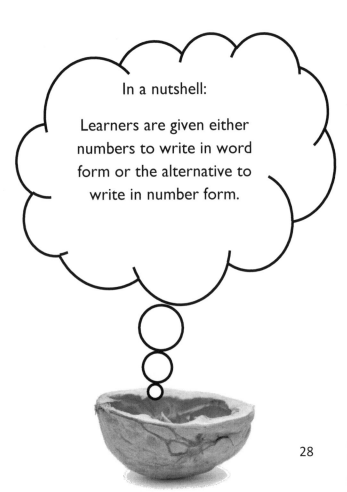

In a nutshell:

Learners are given either numbers to write in word form or the alternative to write in number form.

Example:

Kirendeep's Citizenship learners are researching populations of UK cities. When learners have found a number, they are asked to write the number using words. For example:

Population of Leicester

329,839

Written as: Three hundred and twenty nine thousand, eight hundred and thirty nine.

Population of Nottingham

310,837

Written as: Three hundred and ten thousand, eight hundred and thirty seven.

'Old-School Time'

In a nutshell:

How many of your learners can tell the time on a 'real' watch?

Learners use analogue timings throughout tasks.

Example:

At the start of Tracey's class, she explains a task to learners and asks them what their start time is. Following this she tells them how long they have to complete the task before asking them what their finish time should be.

Tracey: "Using the clock on the wall, who can tell me what time it is?"

Learners: "11:55"

Tracey: "Correct, you have 15 minutes to complete the task. What time should you finish?"

Learners: "12:10"

'Peer SP&G Check'

In a nutshell:

At the end of a written task, learners swap their work with a peer for assessment. At the same time, learners check one another's SP&G.

Example:

Helen asks her Health and Social Care learners to write a statement explaining the roles and responsibilities of a health worker. Upon completion of the task she asks learners to swap their work with a partner. The partners are tasked with checking and giving feedback on the work for spelling, grammar and punctuation in addition to feeding back on the content. Learners then redress their work based upon the peer feedback.

'Quiz Time'

In a nutshell:

Learners work in small groups to create a revision quiz for their peers. They identify the questions, answers and points available.

Example:

Sarah asks her Science learners to work in pairs to create a minimum of five questions on protein synthesis.

They create the question, ensuring that it is clear and concise for peers to understand. They must also know the answer themselves, whilst allocating an appropriate amount of points to each question.

The pairs then take it in turns to ask and answer questions related to the topic in a competitive manner in order to acquire the most points.

'Real or Not?'

In a nutshell:

Learners are given
statements and must
determine whether they
are real or not (true/false).

Example:

Geoff provides his Painting and Decorating learners with a series of statements to determine whether they are real or not real. For example:

"Sandpaper is the most common type of abrasive used in decorating".

"Strings, treads and risers belong to scaffolding".

"Red and brown mix together to make orange".

The activity could be extended further by including spelling, grammar and punctuation errors for learners to identify and correct.

'Scrabble'

In a nutshell:

Learners are given Scrabble tiles to identify key concepts from the lesson. Learners compete to achieve the highest scoring words.

Example:

As a recap activity, Margaret asks her learners to recap all of the key utensils they used during their induction to the kitchen whilst on their Hospitality and Catering course.

Learners create as many words as they can and compete to score the highest points using as many letters as they require. Learners could be stretched by limiting the number of letters they have.

'Twenty Word Challenge'

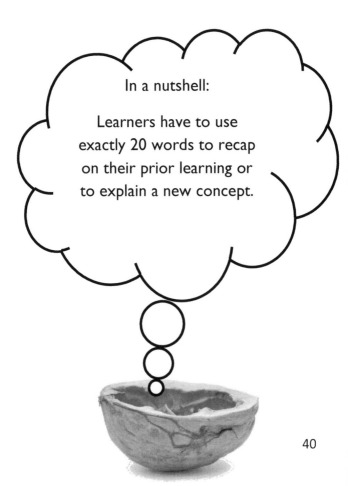

In a nutshell:

Learners have to use exactly 20 words to recap on their prior learning or to explain a new concept.

Example:

Dan starts his session with an image relating to the topic of the day. Learners are tasked with using exactly 20 words to write what the image means/represents for them. Learners are awarded points for exactly twenty words, for the sentence(s) making sense and for correct spelling, punctuation and grammar. This creates a bit of competition.

20 Word Challenge – What does this image symbolise?

'Units of Measurement'

In a nutshell:

Learners are tasked with identifying the correct units of measurement and using alternative units to stretch them further.

Example:

Glen's Plastering learners are calculating the area of a wall. They measure the length and width in metres in order to calculate the area in m^2 before then being tasked with converting this to centimetres.

Upon calculating the area, they are stretched to write the answer using alternative units of measurement. For instance:

Length: 6.43m

Width: 3.49m

Area = 6.43m x 3.49m =22.44m²

This can also be written as 224400cm²

'Vocational Terms'

In a nutshell:

Learners create their own glossary for use in lessons. The glossary includes all technical terms related to their subject.

Example:

Matt provides each of his Construction learners with an empty glossary at the start of the term. Whenever a new technical term is used within the session, Matt asks his learners to write the term in their glossary, provide a definition and use the term in an appropriate sentence. Over the course, learners build up a bank of key words associated with their subject.

Term	Definition	Use
Cladding	Non load-bearing wall covering the exterior wall of a building.	The cladding was made of plastic.
Flashing	Strips of waterproof material which make joints waterproof.	The flashing was used at the roof and wall joint to direct the flow of water.

'Word Link'

In a nutshell:

Learners are given a series of words related to a topic and are tasked with explaining the link between each word.

Example:

Vickie is teaching Human Biology and gives learners a list of body parts on individual hexagons. The learners are tasked with making a link between key words by using a sentence to explain how they link. For example:

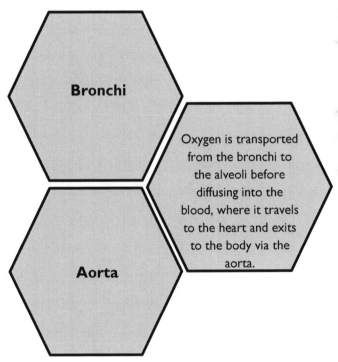

Bronchi

Aorta

Oxygen is transported from the bronchi to the alveoli before diffusing into the blood, where it travels to the heart and exits to the body via the aorta.

'Xplain Yourself'

In a nutshell:

Learners are given thought provoking problems and are asked to explain to the group what their answer is and why.

Example:

Tina is teaching her learners about The Equality Act and provides them with the 9 protected characteristics.

Learners are tasked with ranking each characteristic in order of importance, before explaining their thoughts on why they feel that one characteristic is more important than another.

Learners must be able to provide a rationale as to why they are arguing for a particular point.

'Yin/Yang, Skim/Scan'

In a nutshell:

Learners are encouraged to use different methods of speed reading depending on given tasks.

Example:

Phil's learners are taught to read quickly to determine useful research for their assignments. Phil teaches two quick reading strategies to learners, skimming and scanning.

Learners are taught to skim in order to get a general idea of a research paper, whereas they are taught to scan an article if looking for specific facts or pieces of information to help them with their work.

Learners are encouraged to read a range of texts in order to develop the skill of reading quickly.

'Zap the Waffle'

In a nutshell:

Learners are required to edit their work in order to develop concise writing skills.

Example:

Janette's Hairdressing learners have been asked to produce a write-up of the practical work they completed in a session. Upon completion, they are asked to do a word count before being challenged to remove a percentage of the words depending on ability.

Learners are asked to edit their work by removing 10% of the words used. In order to do this, they calculate the percentage before attempting to reduce the 'waffle' in their writing to achieve the new target.